Charles Robert Ashbee

From Whitechapel to Camelot

Charles Robert Ashbee

From Whitechapel to Camelot

ISBN/EAN: 9783337339371

Printed in Europe, USA, Canada, Australia, Japan

Cover: Foto ©Lupo / pixelio.de

More available books at **www.hansebooks.com**

From
WHITECHAPEL
to CAMELOT

BY
C·R·ASHBEE·
Illustrated by
M·or·IV·

Published by the Guild of Handicraft
(Essex House Mile End Road) London
1892·

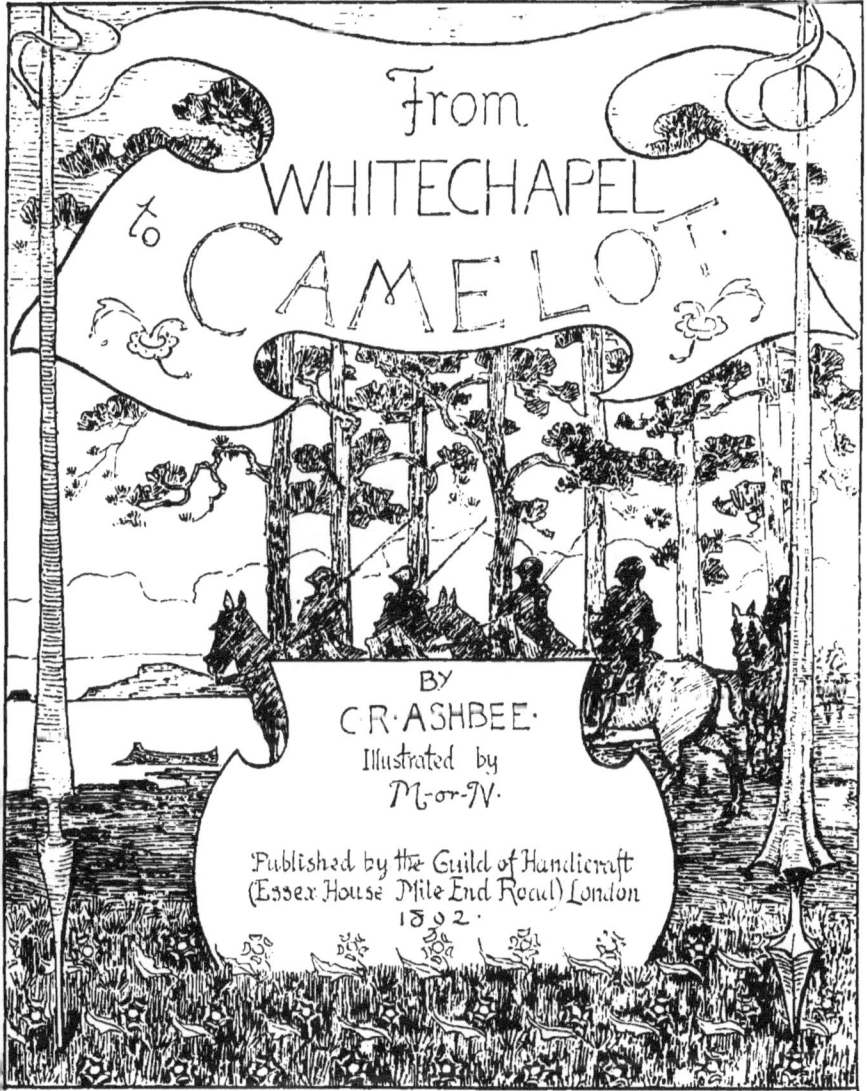

DEDICATED TO THE
FIVE BOYS OF THE
FIRST RIVER
EXPEDITION.

CHAPTER I.

"GOOD luck have thou with thine honour: Ride on because of the word of Truth, of meekness, of righteousness, and thy right hand shall teach thee terrible things."

That was what the old monk was chanting in the forest. It wasn't very clear but if you paid attention to the pauses of his sentences, and to his deep voice as it rose and fell, you could catch everything distinctly.

Willie had left his playmates, the other boys, and was wandering alone by himself thinking of all the strange and great things that might be in 'some day time' when the chant came upon him. He held his breath and listened. After the old monk had finished he went up to him and spoke.

"I want to be a great knight and do great things."

"Well," said the old monk, "there isn't much of you to do it with, and it will take you some years till you grow up, you know, and by that time you'll have got through all your adventures."

"That's all very well," said Willie, "but one may as well begin young if one wants to. Mayn't I begin young?"

"That's for you to say," said the old monk.

"All right, I'll begin young. Tell me please, where can I get the suit of yellow armour and the enchanted sword?"

"Bless me!" said the old monk "it would take two of you to fit into the suit of yellow armour. Why, you're only an ell high."

"What does that matter. Let me try it on first and see, if it doesn't fit me I'll put it back in the box, because, you see they always start well in adventures, and who would set out in knicker-bockers and cap and collar to walk through the enchanted wood? One must have something that shines, at least."

"All right," said the old monk, "the princess Serenity shall dress you."

"Thanks, I can dress myself; besides, I don't want to have anything to do with princesses, in fact, I don't believe in them, but, but, please Mr. Monk *must* there be princesses?"

"That depends what you go for," said the old monk, "if you go for princesses, you'll find them, if you don't, you won't."

"Very well, then I won't," said the boy, "I'll go for my friends."

"What friends?" asked the monk.

"King Arthur and Sir Launcelot."

"Bless me!" said the monk. "It'll take you a long time before you find *them*, besides they've quarrelled, and one broke faith with the other."

"I don't believe it," said the boy, "I believe it was all a horrid fib of someone, and if I catch that someone, I shall give him a good lapping up. Anyway, I shall set off and try and find them, and get them to make it up."

The old monk laughed. "It isn't so easy to get people to make it up," he said. "Are you afraid of giants?"

"I'm not sure," said the boy, "that depends on their size doesn't it?"

"Do you believe in giants?" said the monk.

"Well I suppose I ought to, but I've never seen any."

"Do you think it necessary to see before you believe?" said the old monk.

"You shouldn't ask catchy questions," said the boy, "much better help a fellow do his work! Besides I want to begin."

So Willie put on the armour and lo! it fitted him! Why, he couldn't make out, because as it had been the very suit made for the Earl of Warwick in Edward the Third's reign, it was really much too large for him. But somehow it fitted him and he girded on the sword with the belt covered with gems and the cloak with the cross upon it. His cap he kept, letting the end of it peep out under his casque and thus equipped he went out to seek for his friends.

"Won't you say goodbye to me," said the old monk.

"Of course I will if you like," said the boy, "but won't you come along with me?"

"No," said the old man, sadly, "I couldn't walk so springy as you. But we're friends aren't we? Do you know what friends are?"

"Of course I do," said Willie.

"Then don't lose them," said the old monk.

"It isn't a question of losing them," said the boy, "it's a question of finding them."

"Ah," said the old monk, and bent down his head in thought.

· Willie gave him his hand. The old monk looked at it, pressed it, then drew it up slowly to his mouth, bent his shrivelled face over it, and kissed it.

"Don't cry," said Willie. "'Tisn't half like a man to cry. Besides, we shall meet again."

"Would you really like us to meet again?" asked the old monk.

"I should just think so," said the boy.

"Then we shall," said the old monk.

"How?" said Willie. "What's your call? Tell me, then I shall know. Mine goes like this":—and tossing his head back he shouted a double noted treble into the forest—"Huey! huey! huey! huey!" that was how it sounded. "Now if you'll shout yours I shall know when you are near."

"Mine's a wish," said the old monk.

"What's that?" said the boy.

"If you wish for me at the cross roads I shall be handy. Do you know how to wish?" asked the old monk.

"I should jolly well think I did," said Willie. "But you can't wish *out loud*, you can only wish *inside*, and that's not loud enough to make a man hear."

"Well, if you wish for me *inside*, at the cross roads I shall be handy.

"All right," said the boy, "I will."

"Goodbye then," said the old man, "and if you ever do get to my time of life remember that friends are very scarce—very scarce," the old man repeated, and, drawing his fingers through the boy's hair as he pushed back his head, he kissed him on the forehead and bade him adieu.

CHAPTER II.

AND so Willie went into the forest. It was all lovely pines at
first : great tall trees just as you read of them in the German
fairy tales, and the scent of their barks was warm and
sweet. "It's very beautiful," thought Willie, "but it's sure not to
be a German fairy tale forest right through because I'm not a
German knight; but no doubt other things will happen, we shall see!"

He felt for his sword, it was there, his casque, his cloak. He
looked very fine, and he knew it. It was a coat of bright yellow
armour, splendidly greaved. The enchanted sword was jewelled at
the hilt with blue stones, and round his neck hung a chain of roses
and rings also of blue stones. The belt, too, was made of roses,
square roses, and the circular rings in between. When the sun
shone upon it, it all flashed ; in fact he looked like a bit of sunbeam
gone astray and walking about with a will of its own.

After a little while he heard the sound of horses and wheels, and
a carriage drove up. Inside sat the most charming little elderly
lady possible. She was all dressed in grey and her grey hair
sparkled in the light. Her face was beautifully cut, and she looked
all of a twinkle had it not been for the touch of sadness that lay on
her forehead. The little lady bowed to Willie and he gave her a
royal salute back. He was a little shy, because this was not the
sort of thing that he had expected. The little lady came to his
assistance.

"Very glad to meet you," she said, and she stretched her hand.

"So am I to meet you," said Willie. Then there was a pause.
"I beg your pardon for asking, but are you one of the great ladies
of society that one reads of in the papers. ?"

" No, I'm the little lady in grey," was the answer " and I'm very particular whom I meet."

" But, you can't help meeting people," said Willie, doubtfully.

" Quite so," said the lady, " but one needn't be introduced to them, much less know them."

Willie didn't think he quite understood this, but it might seem rude to ask, and so he stored it up to think it over later.

" And what is *your* name ? " asked the little lady. " Have you got one."

" Of course I have," said Willie.

" What is it then ? "

Willie told her.

" Oh, I don't mean that sort of name," said the little lady. " That sort of name is a mere fluke. The names that people are christened or called by, aren't real names, you know. They only have to have *them* for convenience. It was a mere fluke that you were christened Willie, for instance."

" No, I was christened Willie after my grand dad," said the boy.

" And what was he christened after ? " asked the little lady.

Willie didn't know.

" You see," she said " those sort of names are the merest chances. You might have been christened Charley, or Frank or Walter, but it wouldn't have made any difference to you, would it now ? People and their names are quite separate really, though they don't think so. The only true names are the names I give them. Let me see," she said, " What name shall I give you ? "

She thought for a minute, and then said, " Suppose I call you Sir Percival. Do you think you could wear the name of Sir Percival."

Willie just thought he could. It was such a fine one, besides he knew Sir Percival was one of King Arthur's knights.

" It all depends," she said smartly, reading his thoughts, " it all depends. If you can do as Sir Percival did, I'll let you bear his name, if not, you'll lose it."

" Tell me what to do to keep it," said Willie.

" Sir Percival was one of the few of Arthur's knights who saw the Holy Grail," said the little lady, " and he saw it because he kept himself quite pure and quite true. If you'll do likewise you may bear his name."

" Thank you," said Willie. " Thank you. I will. I'll keep it always, at least "—for the little lady was looking at him hard—" at least, I'll try to. Please tell me," he said, " as you've thought fit to give me so great a name, do you think I shall be able to keep it always ? "

To this the little lady in grey said nothing, but though she said nothing it was quite evident that she felt something, for all her countenance changed, and the sad little wrinkles were drawn upon her forehead, and her eyes looked far away, like one who has the power to see through a world that has been, and on into a world that might have been. Then in a dreamy way she asked Willie the question,

" Are you fond of sweet music ? "

" Rather," said Willie, " do you know many tunes ? "

" Rather," laughed the lady in grey, repeating the tone of the boy's voice, " and I'll teach you some if you like."

" Do! " said Willie.

So she took him by the hand and they went through the forest together. It was lovely : and the strangest things happened as they went. Everything seemed to bow to her, and everything as it bowed whispered musically. The trees bowed, and the bracken and the long grass. And then the little lady began to hum a tune ; such a strange tune, it didn't seem to have any proper beginning or end, it just went on ; but as it went on, the bees and the insects joined in, and as it grew louder the birds joined in, and took it up in chorus, and then the trees grew musical, and their big branches bent gently up and down, and they joined in. As Willie and the little lady went on everything they passed first made a reverent bow to her and then joined in. They passed a stream, and as soon as the little lady smiled at it singing, it all lit up with sunlight, glittered in its ripples and joined in. And the big willow herbs and wild geraniums that grew at its side, caught up the light in their coloured breasts, bowed and joined in, and it wasn't long before everything all around, sun and light, and shade, and flowers and trees, leaves, and grass, birds, bees and butterflies and all the glittering things that pass by you for a moment and then vanish, joined in and sang. All nature, everything from highest to lowest was singing.

Then the lady made him sit down by her side, and bade him listen.

"You see," she said, "it doesn't take much to set them off, as they have got it in them already. Now, try and remember what they sing, and you'll learn how to sing all the sweetest tunes possible. That's what the great musicians do, they just listen and learn, and then one fine day they start singing themselves, without knowing why, and make music for other people. And that's what God does when He wants to do anything new or create anything new :—He just sits still first, listens, and then it comes ; He does it all by music in this way ; Everything is like a great tune to Him, and He moves and creates everything with music. See! see!" she cried.

Willie looked, and saw four dandylion seeds floating along together. "The music has set them going," said the little lady.

The four dandylion seeds made their bow to her, then rested for a minute on a grass blade ; then the blade rocked and the four seeds floated off. Then one of the four unlinked itself from the other three, floated away into a shady corner of the grass and vanished.

The three others rose up into the air again, looking like tiny gold feathers with the sun through them and danced to the music, till another of the three left, floated alone by itself for awhile and then nestled away somewhere out of sight.

"Each with a will of its own you see," said the little lady.

Then the two that were left went on singing by themselves for a bit, like two friends together in life and wandering about the world together, and there came a breath of singing wind, the merest breath, and they were parted.

"I'm for the sun," sang one seed, and up it shot into a stream of sunlight, and "I'm for the clouds," sighed the other, and off it floated into another direction.

"That's how they all go," said the little lady, "and it's the music that sets them all going."

"Why did they bow to you ?" asked Willie. "And why does everything bow to you ? "

"Because I give them their ideas," said the little lady, "they all come to me for ideas?"

"For what?" asked Willie.

"For ideas," she said, laughing, "would you like an idea?"

"Please, I don't think I quite understand you," said Willie.

"Well," said the little lady. "It isn't a thing you can touch or eat or see. It comes and goes and has a way of its own, and sometimes it seizes hold of you, and carries you along with it, and sometimes it drops you in the mud; and then it says to you, 'now get yourself out of your difficulties and when you're out I'll come to you again,' and then it waits and watches to see what you're made of."

"Aren't they rather dangerous things?" said Willie.

"Well, yes, they are," said the little lady "and they're apt to run off the lines like railway trains; but if there were'nt any about, everything would be like a big pulp, and only just *exist*, you see, in fact nothing would happen at all," she said.

"Oh I shouldn't like that," said Willie, "That would be dull; please may I have an idea?"

"That depends what you give me for it," she said rather archly.

Willie made a calculation in his head as to what it would be the correct thing to offer, felt in his pocket, found he had one-and-threepence, thought again, and then said, rather cautiously,

"If you please could you tell me how much about it would be?"

"Ah," said the little lady, and she laughed right out. "Now you talk like Mr. Simon Magus, that will never do."

Willie forgot who Mr. Simon Magus was, though he thought he recollected having seen his name over a shop in Whitechapel. Anyway, he had made a great mistake, and he looked it. Then he looked at the little lady, as much as to say so, with a please-help-me-out look; and being a kind little lady, and always ready to help anybody who looked thus, she drew his hand into hers and said.

"I'll try to. Can you reason?"

"No," said the boy, for he thought that was the safest thing to say under the circumstances.

"No more can I," said the little lady, "and, therefore, we shall be able to find out the truth together. Now who do you think I am."

" You said you were the little lady in grey," said Willie, and he began to get quite bewildered.

"Yes," said she, "and more than that I'm the mother of your two friends."

Willie looked incredulous, that couldn't be, he thought, because they weren't brothers.

" I'm the mother of everybody who's a hero," said the little lady, quietly.

"Then oh—" said Willie rather awestruck, "if you please will you—"

She cut him short. " They are your heros, are they not ? "

" Yes," said Willie.

"That's quite enough for me, then they're my sons ? "

Willie didn't quite follow this nor did he see how relationships could be made so easily as all that, but he felt that he was in a world where all things were possible, and so he waited to hear what might be told him next, besides he had been taught that if you only believed hard enough things came true, but he doubted this a little.

Then the little lady asked him an awfully hard question.

" What is the difference between a man who is a hero and a man tries to be one ? "

Willie thought a minute and then feeling quite sure of the answer said rather disdainfully.

" Why every difference, the man is a hero has done all his adventures, and become one, while the other fellow hasn't got through yet."

" You're quite wrong," said the little lady. " The other fellow as you call him, is the real hero, and the man who is a hero may or may not be a hero after all."

" I don't see that," said Willie " because who's to say when a man's a hero and when he isn't ? "

" Who's to say when you've passed the sixth standard and when you haven't ? "

" The examiners," said Willie, promptly, he was quite sure about that."

"Wrong again," said the little lady, "because *you* might have passed through it though your papers mightn't. It's a very curious fact that, but it is so, none the less. Now we want to find out the truth, don't we? And we neither of us can reason, can we? And you've asked me for an idea, haven't you? and so I'll just put you one question more. Why are you going in search of your friends?"

"Because I love them very much and want to find them," said the boy simply.

"I thought I wanted to," he added, "and there was just a wee bit of pride in the way he said it. "I thought it was a good idea, and so I went."

"It was I who gave you that idea," said the little lady, "that was the idea I sent you."

This was too much, and Willie felt very small and humbled. Like one of the great knights of old he knelt down before her and then without knowing what he was saying or why he said it, he cried to her, "Let me try to be your son too."

The little lady looked at him very sweetly, kissed him on the forehead and whispered into his ear,

"You too are my son, go your ways and win, and we shall meet again."

CHAPTER III.

SO Willie went his ways, and he felt he'd never been so happy all his life. The sun was shining and he began singing. He knew that Sir Launcelot used to sing " 'tira lira' " when he was happy, but as he did'nt get very far with that, he sang the Vicar of Bray, and the Marseillaise and a little tune of Queen Elizabeth's time that his friends had taught him, and then some of the strange tunes that he seemed to have picked up from the little lady came to him ; any way he was very happy.

Oh 'tis good to walk through the bracken four feet high, with the sun shining through the forest, and you feeling yourself a part of all around you. You belong to it, and it belongs to you. And then the trees with their great arms rocking to you and bless-ing you.

Suddenly he saw the boughs swing, and something black hanging on them threatening to impede his passage. He looked, and it was a little black demon with red and green eyes. A horrid little brute. Like a Japanese lacquer figure curled up and leering.

" What are you doing up there ? " said Willie, who thought it his duty to interfere in a case of this sort.

" What are you doing down there ? " said the demon.

" That's no business of yours," said Willie.

" Oh, yes it is," said the demon.

" Who are you ? " said Willie,

" You ? " answered the demon.

" Don't you try and check me," said Willie, " or you'll get the worst of it."

B

" Boo, boo, boo," said the demon, and he swung himself saucily on the bough. " I'm just as big as you, I'm just as strong as you, and I can talk just as tall as you. The only difference is that you're yellow and I'm black ; besides I know more about you than you think. I know what's inside you, and that's more than you know of me."

Willie scarce knew whether to be offended or amused at this, he thought for a minute, and then determined to be amused. Besides there was something in the little black demon that looked friendly and sociable like, and he seemed to recognise his face. Indeed, he felt almost inclined to shake hands with him and become pals, but but he *was* so black and ugly.

" How do you know what *is* inside me ? " asked Willie, " What *is* inside me, then ? "

" *I* am," said the demon, " sometimes."

" Why you said just now you were as big as me."

" Oh, I can sqeeze myself very small," said the demon. " And oh, it's such fun you know, I can make people think that they haven't got me in them at all, when all the time I'm sitting in the corner of their hearts, hammering in nails, tightening them up as hard as I can. Bah ! " said the demon, " I hate a soft heart, it's so bulgey."

" Then you belong to other people besides me," said Willie.

" Oh dear no," said the demon. " I don't belong to anybody, and I don't own anybody, except everybody who is anybody in particular. Do you understand me ? " asked the demon.

" Not quite," said Willie guardedly, because he wasn't sure if the demon was trying to make a fool of him.

" Well then, never mind about the other people," said the demon, " but consider yourself only, in so far as *you* are *you*, you belong to me," Now do you see it ?

" I like that," Willie pouted defiantly. " It's for me to say whom I belong to, I should think."

The demon chuckled at this, and all he said was " *tall, tall, tall,*" and wriggled himself on the bough.

" If you're such an important person that you know what's inside people, I suppose you don't mind telling me your name."

B 2

" It's not a bit of use my telling you my name," said the demon.
" It's a very long one and you'd forget it, and it's hard to pronounce."
" Is it a Japanese name ? " asked Willie.

" Not exactly," said the demon. " Though I've no doubt they
have it there too. Have you visited Japan ? " said the demon
turning the conversation.

" No," said Willie. " But I've seen pictures of you in the British
Museum by Japanese artists, and so I thought you came from
there."

" No," said the demon, loftily. " No, not necessarily, I *have* sat
for a nitchkie before now, but you know," and he said this with a
bewitching society smile, "artists are such imaginative people and
take liberties with your personality," and he waved his hand grandly.

" Well, now, out with it," said Willie. " Who are you, because
I want to be getting on, and I can't stay here all day ? "

" Reflex Personality Esquire," said the demon, magnificently,
"and you'll find me rather harder to get rid of than you think,
good day."

And the demon was gone.

Willie went on through the forest.

" That was not as nice an adventure as some," he said to himself.
" How horrid ! it makes one feel quite creepy, I wonder where the
little beast is now." And then he went on thinking, and then his
thoughts answered him, and they said, " no doubt, no doubt you do,
no doubt, no doubt ; tall ! tall ! tall ! "

CHAPTER IV.

WILLIE wandered on and soon he came to a hilly part of the forest. Up hill and down dale, then he came to some cross roads, and at their meeting was a sign post.

"Which way should I go now?" he thought; then he remembered the old monk said if he wished for him at the Cross Roads he would come and help. "But no," thought Willie, "it's rather early in the day to ask for help. I'll try and do it by myself a bit first." Then he looked at the sign post, and one hand had this written on it, "To the Mountain of Facts." "That is sure to be my way," said Willie, "and I shall find my friends there."

It wasn't long before he came to the foot of the mountain and he girt himself up for the ascent. It was rather heavy walking, and they didn't seem to keep the roads very well in these parts, lots of loose stones and boulders. It was evident that the little lady in grey didn't drive about much here.

Up he went, however, along the mountain side, when he came to something that looked like a house, a large house, at the roadside. As the door was ajar Willie peeped in and saw a room that he thought he knew, only it was so much larger. But in the room was a strange sight indeed. "A giant, a very giant at last," thought Willie. "And yet I've seen that old fellow before in Stratford, what a beastly brute he looks, though, when you see him all by himself, and I'd no notion he was this size. Why what on earth is he doing?"

Willie peeped through the door into the giant's house. He looked and listened.

There sat Giant Grumbold, the workman, his pipe in his mouth, and a pot of beer by his side. He looked very lazy and yet not too lazy to growl and snarl at himself. "He's not very particular about his dress, either, the dirty fellow," thought Willie, "and as for his tools, I should like to know how he's ever to do a respectable day's work if he keeps them in that condition, why all the edges of the planes must be blunted in that sack of his." But Grumbold didn't seem to mind about his tools. Dirty he was, certainly, "but if he's been at work that don't matter," though Willie, "anyway."

Grumbold wore his bowler on the back of his head, and had on a rather shabby frock coat, while round his neck was a mottled red cloth. As for his boots and trousers it was quite certain he hadn't cleaned them for a week. "I can't think how anyone would give him a job in that condition at all, but I have seen him more respectable than this," said Willie to himself. "I'll say that for him."

But what on earth was he doing. It was strange indeed. In front of Giant Grumbold was a big pie, and in it a knife and fork. Every now and then he would make an effort to cut himself a bit of the pie and taste it, and then as soon as he had got half way, he got very angry with himself for doing it, and threw the knife and fork aside again.

Omitting the ornamental oaths, and the short but improper adjectives that came in front of the nouns without any apparent connection, this was the sort of conversation that Grumbold was holding with himself :

"I *will* have it," and he stuck the knife in. "When a man's hungry he's got to *eat*," and so saying he took a long swig from his mug. "Didn't I say I was going to save it for *afterwards*," and then he cursed himself and looked as if he wanted to eat himself up rather than the pie. "Get along –yer—yer—yer." "What's the use of having the thing here when it's got to be *eaten*," he said, and then he made another lunge at the pie, then he stamped and looked at the fork, and then he cursed the fork horribly. "No, I *won't* eat you, there—take *that*," and then he kicked the pie.

" He seems to think he's doing the pie a favour by not eating it,"
thought Willie, " I wonder if the pie minds."

The pie evidently didn't mind, because the string of curses that
followed upon this rupture between the pie and himself was perfectly
dreadful and the pie took no notice.

" It's the knife," growled Grumbold.

" No it's not," said Willie, half out loud, "The knife's got nothing
to do with it."

Then Grumbold growled again and gave himself a thump on the
head. " Come now, that's better," thought Willie. " If he'll only
go on finding fault with himself and not with his tools he may get a
little more reasonable."

But he didn't, he got more unreasonable; he stood up and
groaned, and then he sat down and groaned, and then he said it
wasn't fair, and then he got up and walked about, and then he made
another dig at the pie, and then he put the pie into the cupboard,
locked it, and threw away the key, and then he grew furious at
having done this, swore he would eat the pie for what anybody said
to him, took a great crowbar out of his tool bag and broke open the
cupboard. " Poor chap," thought Willie, " he really does not seem
to know what he wants, but if he's as bad as this when he's sober,
what must he be like when he's drunk. Perhaps he's under a spell,
that's an idea now, let's see if I can help him," and so saying
Willie pushed open the door and entered the room.

" Good day, sir, can I do anything for you," asked Willie. " You
seem in trouble."

" Who are you ? " said Grumbold, looking down on the small
knight in coloured armour who stood on the threshold before him.
" Can't you leave a poor fellow alone ? "

" I've seen you in Stratford, Mr. Grumbold, I recognised you by
your red whiskers, and as you seemed in trouble I thought I might
help."

" Yes," said Grumbold, " have you got a shilling about yer ? "

" A shilling won't help him much," thought Willie, " but if that's
really all he wants to get him out of his trouble, he may as well

have it. Let me see," he felt in his pocket, found he had one and threepence, and handed Grumbold the shilling. Grumbold took it, looked at it, and then swore.

" What's the good of giving a man a shilling when they take from him home and comforts, they live on the blood and sorrow of the working man they do, and then they offer him a shilling ! "

" Well, I only did what you asked me," said Willie.

" Look here," said Grumbold, " I'll tell you what I shall do," and Grumbold shook his head with determination, " I shall *strike!*"

" That's an idea now," said Willie. " They often win in strikes. I've done picketing in a strike before now. I'll help you if you like. Who's the company ? " asked Willie, for he was up in those things.

" Dearn the company ! " said Grumbold, " what I'm thinking of is the pie."

" You've got the pie," said Willie, " it's no use striking for it."

" What's the good of having the pie when I've no appetite to eat it ! "

" That's true," said Willie, " but then you could save it till you have."

" What's the use of saving a thing that's intended to be eaten ! "

" Won't it keep ? " asked Willie.

" Of course it will keep," said the workman, " but think of the trouble and expense of keeping it. Haven't I got my rent to pay?"

" I suppose you have," said Willie. " But everybody's got to do that, however unpleasant it is."

" Unearned inkriment, that's what I call it," said Grumbold. " Unearned inkriment, and it isn't fair on a fellow to make him want to have his pie and make him want to eat it too."

" I think you're rather an unreasonable chap, Mr. Grumbold, if you don't mind my saying so."

Grumbold grew very red at this, and his eyes regularly bulged out of his head. " Look here," he said," if you ever say that again to a man of my position, a respectable working man, who has as much as he can do to keep house and home together, let alone rent and rates and taxes, and you a young shaver, who has nothing better to do than go loafing about the world like a blooming cheese-cake, if you *hever* say that again," and here Grumbold piled on the H's, " I'll, I'll, I'll give you such a basting that you won't forget in a hurry—to say that to me—too—me, a cove as ought to be endowed by the state, ME ! mind if you hever say that again, I'll, I'll, I'll——" and therewith shaking his great pipe at Willie, he strode away out of the house in a towering rage.

CHAPTER V.

WHEN the giant was fairly gone Willie went on his way. " I quite forgot to ask him if he'd seen King Arthur and Sir Launcelot," he said to himself, "and as he seemed to live about here, and must have seen them pass he might have known. but I don't know though, he seemed so taken up with his own concerns, that he probably wouldn't have known. No, I believe he's an old brute," said Willie, "that he is."

Up the high road of the mountain of Facts went Willie. It was rather hard and rather hot, and he wished he were coming to the end of it. " I've got to get over it though, I suppose," and so he trudged on his way pluckily, till he came to a cross road and then feeling very lonesome and tired he set to and wished for the old monk.

The old man was as good as his word, for, hardly was the wish accomplished when he appeared, staff in hand at the corner of the road, chanting his psalm. " Ride on in the word of truth,"—

" How did you get up this great big hill ? " asked Willie.

" I have ways of my own," was the answer, "not known to other folk. A sort of private right of way."

" Will you show it to me ? "

The old Monk laughed. " No," said he, "no, that's a thing every man must find for himself. Do you know that it's the correct thing for people who want to get the other side to walk up the mountain of Facts by themselves."

" Wouldn't it save a great deal of labour if they were to tunnel the mountain ? " asked Willie.

"Oh, no doubt, and that's what some of the engineers and men of science are always trying to do, but it's very funny they always get wrong in their calculations and have to begin over again."

"What a poor set of crocks they must be here," said Willie rather contemptuously, "Why don't they put a London man on the job, he'd do it."

"Might be," said the old monk, "but he'd be a very clever fellow if he did do it. How are you getting on, laddie, you want me to help you?"

"Well," said Willie, not exactly liking to own it, "I'm rather tired and want to be at the top, and I thought you were the sort of chap, who might give a fellow a hint."

"Well, I will," said the old monk. "The secret of this mountain is, that everything is double on it. The stones are double, and the trees are double, and the people you meet on it, double. You see it's the mountain of facts, and every fact is double, that is to say it has its side that you *can* see and its side that you *can't* see. And as soon as you quite get to understand this you'll find that every step you take up the hill is double as big as you thought it was, and so you get up to the top in half the time."

Willie didn't think he understood it at all, but the old monk was a wise old fellow so he made up his mind to try and understand, or at least have a good look at the stones and things as he went along to see if he couldn't save himself a bit of journey.

"That's all I have to say now," said the monk, "good-bye." And off he went, slowly, down the hill, chanting to himself. Willie went on his way again a little brighter perhaps, at having something new to think over, and looking about him at everything by the wayside. He hadn't gone far when a gentleman in a tall hat and a long frock coat came hurrying down the mountain road.

"Good day," said the gentleman, in the tall hat, "I'm glad to see you. My name is Mr. Pushington, I live in Kensington and I'm a member of Parliament."

Willie remembered driving through Kensington sometimes, on an omnibus, a place with big red houses, but rather formal, and there were no Italian ice grinders in the summer and no chestnut hawkers in the winter, and that made it dull, but he didn't remember that he had ever seen Mr. Pushington. People in frock coats and top hats were very much alike, unless you happened to know them well. However, the man seemed friendly and so Willie offered him his hand.

"I'm in a great hurry," said Mr. Pushington, "I always am, but I must stop to have a chat with you."

"Come now, that's kind of him," thought Willie.

"It's one of my principles in life, never to let an opportunity go by," said Mr. Pushington. Why he, Willie, should be one of Mr. Pushington's opportunities, didn't seem quite clear but doubtless things would explain themselves. But why shouldn't he turn the tables and make one of Mr. Pushington.

"Can you help me to find my friends, King Arthur, and Sir Launcelot?" said Willie.

"Well," said Mr. Pushington drily, "I don't think you'd care for them much from me, I only keep them bound."

"What, keep them bound!—in a dungeon?" and Willie was martial at once, at the thought of a possible rescue.

"Dear me, no," said Mr. Pushington. "In a book, of course—in a book with gilt edges and morocco leather. I like to see everything in its place, and there worth a good binding don't you think?"

"I don't mean like that," said Willie. "I mean the real men."

"Oh, I see," said Mr. Pushington. "Of course, I beg your pardon. I forgot that there were 700 years between you and me. I might have seen that by your costume. However, I take no count of time and space, I live in the nineteenth century, and deal in telegraphs and steam engines."

"Then perhaps you're a manufacturer?"

"That's exactly what I am," said Mr. Pushington. "The whole world is my big machine and I move it."

This seemed to Willie rather a large order, even for a big manufacturer, and he looked a bit incredulous.

"Oh you needn't shake your head," said Mr. Pushington, "perhaps you'd like me to convince you. Look here," and Mr. Pushington opened a little black bag that he carried, and fetched out a long

parti-coloured tube, with glass at both ends, but smaller at the end
where you put your eye. On the outside was painted, "P. Pushington " and " A present for a good boy. International Exhibition,
1851."

" Hold it up to your eye and click it round by degress," said Mr.
Pushington. Willie did so, and what a strange and wonderful thing
it was when you looked through it. First there were thousands of
bits of glass set into patterns, then he turned it with a click, and
the thousand bits of glass changed into a thousand great cities, each
seeming to smoke and flash fire and vapours from itself, then another
click and Willie's vision became clearer, he still saw all the great
cities, but he saw what was going on in them, too. Thousands of
men and women, hurrying to and fro with great instruments and
tools, hammering, sawing, banging, filing, planing, and moving
great machines up and down, up and down, and turning steam
whistles off and on. But though he looked very carefully, no result
seemed to come of it all.

" Isn't that lovely ? " said Mr. Pushington. " You're at a most
interesting part of it now." Willie clicked again, and all the cities
changed into ships, and each ship was laden with bales full of
rubbish, and steaming over a great ocean ; then another click, and
the thousand ships turned into a thousand shorthand clerks,
scribbling away notes for dear life.

" Have you got to the press representatives ? " asked Mr. Pushington,
excitedly. " Aren't they awfully nice, don't you think ? "

Willie clicked again, and then he seemed to see bits of ships, and
bits of shorthand writers, and bits of cities, and bits of work shops :
and each bit had a string tied to it, and a man in the background
was jerking them up and down.

" Who is it ? " said Willie.

" Click again, and see," said Mr. Pushington, and Willie clicked.

" Why, it's you," said Willie. But before he had time to look at
the smile of pathetic benevolence that lit Mr. Pushington's face, the
kaleidescope gave another click, and Willie cried out, " Why, it's
Giant Grumbold ! "

" Dear, dear," said Mr. Pushington, "there must be some mistake, give it to me." And, taking the kaleidescope, he looked through it, clicked it round several times, put it in his bag quickly, and changed the subject.

" Do you play games ? " he asked.

" Don't I just," said Willie. " But I like them best when there are sides, and lots of chaps join in."

" So do I," said Mr. Pushington, " how odd."

Willie looked at Mr. Pushington and thought to himself, " Well, he wouldn't be able to run far, in that hat." But it wouldn't have been a polite thing to say, so he asked him, " What's your favourite game ? "

" Politics," said Mr. Pushington.

" Easy there," said Willie, " don't you try and best me. I know what politics are."

" Do you, though," said Mr. Pushington. " That's more than I do. Politics has sides like any other game, hasn't it ? "

" All right," said Willie. " Which side are you on ? "

" Both," said Mr. Pushington.

" How can you be on both sides of the game at once? And what if there be more than two sides, there now ? " said Willie, not to be done. " Are you Tory, or Liberal, or Radical, or Socialist ?

" I'm a philosophical mugwump," said Mr. Pushington, calmly.

" What's that ? " said Willie.

" You shouldn't ask such embarrassing questions. It's not good manners to ask questions like that of politicians, except—except when they're on platforms," added Mr. Pushington.

" Sorry," said Willie. " I didn't mean any offence, but may I know why ? "

" Certainly," said Mr. Pushington. " The reason's obvious. It's because we're all such humbugs."

" Is every politician a humbug ? " asked Willie.

" Certainly," said Mr. Pushington, " that's one of the rules of the game."

" Then what's the game for ? " asked Willie.

" Don't you even know that?" said Mr. Pushington. " I thought
every English boy knew that. And to think of your get-up, too—
why, to make laws for the country, of course, and to talk about
things."

" Yes, but it's wise talk," said Willie. " Isn't it ? "

" Oh, of course," said Mr. Pushington, " though you might not
think it, and thought it don't always come to anything. But it's
just this," said Mr. Pushington, "things go on perfectly well whether
people play at politics or not. I see to that, and (Mr. Pushington
hesitated a moment) so does Mr. Grumbold."

" Oh, you know Mr. Grumbold, do you ? " said Willie, pleased at
finding a common topic for conversation.

" I should rather think I did," said Mr. Pushington, pensively, he's
a very great friend of mine ; he works my big machine for me. You
want a big man to work a big machine, don't you ? "

" Isn't Mr. Grumbold rather hard to get on with ? " said Willie.

" H'm," said Mr. Pushington, " well, yes and no. It depends how
you work him, he's all right by himself, but I object to his principles,
or rather, his principle, for he only has one."

" What's that ? " asked Willie.

" His union," said Mr. Pushington, with a sigh. " If I could
only have him without his principles, they do upset my machine so
dreadfully, sometimes. He belongs to ' The Habitual-Strikers'-Pie-
Keepers'-and-Eaters'-and-General-Labourers'-Union,' and they
amuse themselves sometimes by pulling out the screws of my big
machine, and it takes ever so long to put it to rights again."

This struck Willie as being a new form of union tactics, unfamiliar
to him. But before he could ask any question, Mr. Pushington had
already babbled on.

" Well, well," said Mr. Pushington, " I must be off. I've got to
go to the House."

" In Kensington ? " asked Willie.

" No, in Westminster," said Mr. Pushington. " That's where I
play my game."

" What do you do at the House ? " asked Willie.

" I'm engaged in private bill legislation," said Mr. Pushington.

C 2

" Is that a paying business ? " asked Willie.

" I fancy some people find it so," said Mr. Pushington courteously, " but oh, but it's a very long job, a very long job."

" A long job is not usually a disadvantage," thought Willie. " especially if they pay him by time and not by piece."

" A very long job " repeated Mr. Pushington. " You've no idea what a time it takes to get a private bill through."

" How do you do it ? " asked Willie.

" Well," said the M.P. " You've got to do a great deal of wire pulling and you've got to watch your opportunity."

There was something that sounded exciting in the method of this and Willie thought he would like to ask if he might join in the sport when Mr. Pushington pulled out his watch and said,

" Dear, dear, I've got to meet the Archbishop, I must go. Dear, dear, you don't know how difficult it is to pull an Archbishop through. It's ever so much harder to do than giant Grumbold, I've pulled him through many a time before now, though he alway, swears he'll never be wire pulled again. But then his pie you sees you humour him with his pie. You can do a great deal with that pie of his. But these Archbishops they're such tame elephants and they don't have pies, that is of course they have other things. Dear, dear, I don't know if I shall ever pull the Archbishop through, he's such a weight, still I'll try my best. Good-bye." And off went Mr. Pushington, the manufacturer.

" The old monk's quite right," thought Willie. " Everybody's double in this place. I mean not double in the bad sense. being a brute don't you know, all the time you're really smiling at a fellow, but double in what he says and what he does. I wonder why he should be."

The sun was warm and the sky blue. Willie stretched himself on the grass and rested his face on his hands, he wanted to think things out a bit. " Why should everybody be double? I wonder why, I wonder why ? "

" It's not a bit of good wondering." said a voice, and exactly opposite him was a little, ugly, round, black face with green and red eyes, also resting on its hands, and looking straight at him. Willie didn't like this at all. "Can't you leave a fellow alone, when he wants to think a thing out. Go away."

"How do you know, but that I'm helping you to think the thing out?" said the little black demon.

"I'd rather do without your help," said Willie, "I'd rather think by myself."

"You *are* thinking by yourself," said the little black demon, "and you won't get rid of me by being surly to me."

"That might be," though Willie, "and yet to be friendly to him might encourage him," so he tried a middle course.

"You ought to have better manners," said Willie, "and when a man doesn't want your company, you ought to take the hint and go."

"There you're quite wrong," said the demon, "for the beauty of me just is that I come when I'm not wanted. Besides, don't you preach goody goody to me. People often try it on, but it never answers."

"Of course it doesn't, any fool knows that," said another voice, a big, buzzy, snarly, sour voice. Willie looked to see to whom the voice belonged, when a great big horse fly, with mottled brown wings and a black back, settled down besides the demon, and veered one of it's great eyes round at him.

"Permit me to introduce you, ahem! my friend Skugg," said the demon, politely, waving one hand to Willie and one to the fly.

"Glad to meet you, Skugg," said Willie, because, though he wasn't really very glad, he thought it was only polite to make some reply in the usual way.

"I'm a lady," said the horse fly, snappishly, "and I'll trouble you not to be so familiar."

"I beg your pardon, Mrs. Skugg," said Willie. "I didn't mean any offence."

The horse fly made no reply, and only looked as if she thought, "I'd sting him through that yellow armour, if I could, even though it wasn't worth the exertion." Then she levelled her eye round again at the demon.

" Dinner ! " she said. The demon got up and picked a blue geranium, threw it on the ground, and trampled on it till all it's colour was crushed from it; the horse fly crawled towards it, sniffed round it, and then snarled :

" Not dead enough ! pick another."

" It won't be any deader," said the demon.

" Pick another, do as I tell you." The demon did so, and after he'd picked about ten geraniums Willie protested.

" It's a pity to pick all those jolly flowers and spoil them."

" You dry up," said Mrs. Skugg. " What I like is no business of yours."

" It's only a way she has," said the demon. " She never eats half of them, either, but she likes a selection, and she'll come again to-morrow and nibble at them when they're a bit high, and more to her taste."

" You talk about yourself, or not at all," snarled the horse fly.

" My good woman," said the demon, " what's the good of telling me to talk about myself, when I haven't got one ? "

" The horse fly levelled both her eyes on the demon, gave him a very poisonous look, slowly flapped her brown wings, curled up her ugly grey body, and buzzed straight for his ear, stung him horribly, and then shot off like a needle into the forest.

" The beast ! the beast ! " cried the demon, and off he ran as fast as ever he could to take some frightful vengeance.

WHEN the coast was clear Willie took a survey of his surroundings. He found himself lying under an elder bush nicely shaded from the sun. Why it should have been so he could not make out, but it seemed as if the elder bush had spread its arms out there purposely to shelter him and every now and again it fanned some of its green leaves and made a pleasant wind upon his cheeks.

"It's so kind of it," thought Willie, "especially on a hot day like this." And so he lay among the leaves enjoying the wind, the sunshine and the shade.

The elder bush appeared to be musing to himself. "Life *is* large and sunny," he said, "strange that people don't see this, and yet I've told them so often enough, one can't do more than use one's influence," and then he fanned his leaves "socially or otherwise," he added and then he bowed one of his branches in a very dignified way as if he were saluting some great powdered lady of the last century.

"Large and sunny," he mused, "things have gone on, and things will go on—oh! how lovely it all is!—and God is very good to give to His elect so large a margin of leisure."

"Are you one of His elect?" asked Willie, interrupting the soliloquy.

The elder bush expressed great surprise at being asked a question of this kind.

"How could *you*, who wear the coat of armour made for the Earl of Warwick in 1346, ask such a question?" he said.

But Willie didn't want the elder bush to be under any mistake on that score.

"Oh, please I didn't really live then," he said. "I'm not so old as the suit; and I've only got it on for the occasion."

"And pray, what is the occasion that you have got it on for?" asked the bush rather frigidly.

"I'm going through the enchanted wood," said Willie, "and I'm looking for my friends King Arthur and Sir Launcelot."

The elder bush brightened up at this. "My dear sir," he said, "I apologize I might have known that you were one of us. I beg your pardon. I *beg* your pardon most *sincerely*," and thereupon he made another eighteenth century bow.

Willie couldn't see why the elder bush should apologize so profusely, but no doubt he thought "It's because he knows my friends."

"Manners maketh man" murmured the elder bush and he gave another stately bow.

Willie was just about to continue the conversation, when, plump, plump, plump down fell a great green caterpillar from the top of the bush and lit on one of the lower stalks and leaves near by.

"Hullo!" said Willie, "who are you and what do you want?"

"Pray, don't be alarmed," said the green caterpillar, "I'm a mere coincidence. I'm always happening but nobody takes much count of me."

And thereupon he shrunk up and spread out, and shrunk up and spread out, working his stomach up and down till he'd got to the end of the leaf, when, quite forgetting that he was too heavy for it, he lost his balance and toppled over on to the ground.

"Poor chap!" cried Willie, "haven't you hurt yourself?"

It took the caterpillar some time to uncurl, but when he had wriggled into shape again, he said beamily, "No thanks, I'm a mere coincidence, I often happen, nobody much minds and I'm very well padded, thanks all the same."

"It's well enough for you," said a small red money spider gasping for breath, "but it's rather rough luck on a little chap like me when a big hulk of fifty tons comes thundering down upon him!"

The caterpillar smiled again complacently. "Dear friend," he said, "do compose yourself, don't you see I'm a mere coincidence, how can I help it; besides, look what a lovely combination of colour we make. Why you're vermilion and I'm pea green, just think of it!"

In answer to this the little red spider rushed rapidly all over the caterpillar and then rushed back again.

" That's what you're always doing," said the caterpillar, "it doesn't hurt me at all, it's only a little irritating and I'm sure it must tire you, my good soul,"—and here he smiled benignly, "can't you keep still a bit ?"

" No," said the spider and swift as lightning he shot up a grass blade, surveyed the caterpillar all over six times and rushed down again.

" Well then, I'm quite sure you'll die of heart disease some day, that's all I can say, now I've warned you, do take life a bit easier there's a good thing ; for my sake do now if not for your own."

But the little red spider would not be pacified, he rushed all over and about the place, and called up one little red spider, and then another, until at last there were a dozen or more of them rushing here and there, up and down, in and out, hither and thither, in the wildest state of excitement. The caterpillar looked on, not in the least troubled at the confusion he had caused, but mildly remarked :

" How ridiculous these financiers are when they once get into a panic."

The excitement among the spiders increased and spread so rapidly that it woke up the shrew mouse close by, she rustled amid her leaves and peeped out of her hole.

" Dear, dear," she said, " What is it all about ?"

" There," said the caterpillar, "you've woke up the next door tenant, I thought you would ! "

" Dear, dear," repeated the shrew mouse, " what on earth is it all about, is it another crisis ?—these things happen periodically now, it's really most distressing."

" It's really most absurd," said the caterpillar. " Their system's out of order again.   I can't think what's the good of having a system at all, if it's so easily upset."

" I shall appeal to the landlord," said the shrew mouse, " and ask him to interfere, and if he doesn't I shall quit ! "

This threat seemed to have an effect upon the spiders, for they grew quieter at once, some hid under leaves, and some curled themselves up into pellets and pretended to be dead, and some timidly swung on their threads and began spinning again.

Then suddenly six of them made off as fast as possible, in one direction, together.

" Where are they off to now ? " said the shrew monse.

" Don't you see ? " said the caterpillar. " They've found a new tare."

Willie watched and saw them make for a little vetch that was just peeping over the grass.

The vetch didn't seem to like it, for it said, " No, no, you'd much better not, you know I've been sown by the enemy, and I shall get you into dreadful trouble and confusion if you come here. You know I shall."

" There's no stopping them now," said the shrew mouse. " That's what they call enterprise. If they'd only let us have a little more quiet, and not think that the whole scheme of things depended upon their fussing and calculations, we should all be so much happier."

Several other voices, apparently below ground, chimed in at this, and agreed with the shrew mouse ; but the shrew mouse didn't seem inclined to converse with them.

" Who were they ? " asked Willie.

" Oh, merely some of the sub-tenants," said the shrew mouse, " they're of no account."

" Are they mice too ? " asked Willie.

" Dear me, no ! " was the answer. " Merely beetles, grubs, and blind-worms. Permit me——"

" But——" said Willie.

" No, no, no," said the shrew mouse. " Permit me to introduce you to the three gilded ladies who live under yonder leaf, Miss Prospect, Miss Retrospect, and—Etcetera."

" What was the third one's name, please ? " asked Willie.

" She hasn't got one," said the shrew mouse.

" Surely she must have a name," said Willie. " Everybody has a name, even if it's only for convenience—for instance—my name's Willie for convenience, but I've got a much better name than that besides."

" Go and ask her then, sir," said the shrew mouse.

Willie looked up under the bush and saw two gilded flies sitting side by side ; their wings glittered in the dim light of a green leaf, the end of which was curled up and woven together.

" May I know your name ? " asked Willie, politely.

" *I am*," said the fly.

Willie hesitated. " What did you say you were ? "

" I simply *am*," said the gilded fly. " This is my sister Retrospect, and this is my sister Prospect."

" But I only see two of you," said Willie.

" The third one isn't out yet," said the fly.

" Give my love to the stranger," said a little voice in the cocoon at the corner of the leaf. " I shall be born to-morrow, if it's sunny."

" But please." said Willie, " I don't understand. How can there be three of you if one isn't born ? "

" You'd be still more puzzled," said Retrospect, the second fly, " if you knew that I was only pretending to be alive."

" And still more," said the first fly, " if you knew that I had no existence whatever, and that that was the reason for my having no name. But, buz, buz, one's got to talk to you in a very simple way, of course. Have you ever heard of a young lady coming out ? "

" Yes," said Willie.

" Well, she's a young lady before she's out," said the first fly, " isn't she ? "

" Yes," said Willie. " I suppose so."

" And she's a young lady after she's out, isn't she ? "

" Yes," said Willie.

" Well, it's to be hoped she is," said the fly, " so pray be more considerate to my younger sister and don't fancy you know everything."

Willie thought it rather hard to be snubbed like this, but the cocoon comforted him.

" Stranger," it said, " Wait for me to-morrow at mid-day in the sunshine and I'll come to you."

" Friend," said the second fly dreamily, " do you remember how the little lady in grey made the woods sing to you ? Well, I sang alto in that chorus."

" Buz, buz," said the first fly, " that's all much too romantic. Things aren't near so nice as they were once or as they ever will become. Isn't that so ? " she said to Willie.

" I'm sure I don't know, at least I don't think I do."

" Dear, dear, you're very innocent. Now, answer me this," said the gilded fly, " which of the three would you rather have: the holiday, or the prospect of the holiday, or the retrospect of the holiday ? "

" The holiday of course," said Willie.

" Well that's very complimentary to me no doubt," said the gilded fly, " but if I asked you the same question again to-morrow, would you give me the same answer ? "

" Of course I would," said Willie.

" Then don't tell such horrid fibs to-day," said the gilded fly. " If you prefer the prospect of the holiday say so straight and don't beat about the bush ! "

" I knew he'd like me best," said the little voice in the cocoon. " Wait for me to-morrow, kind stranger, and I'll fly to you in the mid-day sunshine."

Willie wondered why the elder bush had taken no share in all this, as it must concern him so nearly, and when the conversation had ceased he spoke to him again and asked him.

The elder bush replied primly :

" I'm the ground landlord and speak another language."

" Oh, you're the landlord, are you ? " said Willie. " Then you'll be able to tell me all about the grubs and blind-worms and —"

But the elder bush cut him short.

" Of course it s very sweet of you," he said, " to take such an interest in my tenants and I love philanthropists above all men, but things go on so nicely here and my agent arranges everything so well, that I'd much rather you let them be. That was what my friend Lord Melbourne always said, and I agree with him. ' Can't you leave it alone ? ' That's what he said, and I agree with him," said the elder bush. " It's a lovely day, isn't it ? " he added, and fanned his branches up and down.

But Willie still had questions that he wanted to have answered. So he remained still and thought. He was wondering why things that were so strange should yet seem so familiar, and why each one of these little creatures should have something in him that he believed he'd met before.

At length when he had thought it out and fitted the question nicely together, he put it to the elder bush.

"You'd better go and ask my friend the nettle, if you want questions of that sort answered. She owns the next estate," said the elder bush. "Only take care how you do it, because she's rather sarcastic sometimes."

Willie saw that the elder bush didn't much like being questioned further, and, thinking it was best not to spoil so pleasant an acquaintance for the sake of a stray bit of information, he thanked the elder bush for his kindness and his introduction and left him.

The nettle was growing hard by, but he didn't invite Willie to rest under him, on the contrary he seemed quite aggressive.

"I know *you!*" he said, "you'd like to cut me down with your sword."

Willie had not had that intention, but the thought came to him that at another time, and under other conditions, a little lashing about among those tall brittle stalks wouldn't be bad exercise. Nettles were nasty things, he had always thought. But of course this was an exceptional nettle; and after all why shouldn't he make friends with it. So he tried to hide up what his feelings were about nettles in general, and simply said :

"No, I wouldn't, I only want to be friends, and I believe you're a very wise person, aren't you, who can answer questions?"

"Mayhap:" said the Nettle. "My name is Karma. 'Tis an Eastern name, but that's where they first found me out in the very early days."

"And did they import you from there?" asked Willie.

"No," said the nettle grimly, "I came quite of my own accord. I always do go alone by myself and nobody tends or cares for me, because nobody loves me."

This made Willie feel quite sad for the nettle. "Has nobody ever loved you?" he asked.

But the nettle took no heed of the question. "Nobody loves me," he said, "and yet I bring good as well as evil sometimes. I follow man, and have followed him for ages, when he journeys to the West I journey with him, when he crosses the sea I cross with him, when he enters the undiscovered country I enter with him, when he builds himself a cottage by the wayside I wait for him outside his garden gate, and when I meet him I *sting* him."

"But why should you?" said Willie.

"Because I'm one of his consequences," said the nettle.

" What's that ? " asked Willie.

" What's an unripe apple after you've eaten it ? " asked the nettle.

" Is it a riddle ? " asked Willie.

" No, it's a precipitated stomach-ache," said the nettle.

" Would you sting me now, if I came very near you ? "

" Certainly," said the nettle.

" Then that would be beastly mean of you, because I've done you no harm."

The nettle shook his tawny head, and answered slowly : " One of man's misfortunes is his forgetfulness—you're like the rest of them—you forget what you did 200 years ago."

" Get along!" said Willie. " Why, I wasn't born then—I'm only fourteen next birthday."

The nettle laughed bitterly. " And so I suppose you think you were born to please yourself ? "

That was a new way of putting things, and had never occurred to Willie before. After all, what *was* he born for ? He didn't in the least know what to answer.

" Very few people do know what they're born for," said the nettle, " and oft-times have I to sting them into knowledge ; but even then they only find out what they might have been born for."

" I know what I want," said Willie, " if that's what you mean ? "

" And what do you want ? " asked the nettle.

" My friends, King Arthur and Sir Launcelot. Can you tell me where to find them ? "

" Yes."

" Where ? "

" Where you least expect them," said the nettle.

Willie wondered whether this was meant to be sarcastic, and he looked as much, but the nettle merely answered, grimly, " No, it's only when I sting I'm sarcastic. You see I remember when King Arthur was on earth, near a thousand years ago, and, as you know, he was to come again. So he did, and people didn't know him but it was he, nevertheless. You were here a thousand years ago, too, but of course you've forgotten all about it—perhaps if I sting you may remember—still I'm not always sarcastic, and so won't sting you. But don't forget, I have a tremendous memory. Now go your ways and find your friends. Where you least expect them, there you will find them.

CHAPTER VII.

TELLS OF THE CONFLICT IN THE VALLEY.

WHEN Willie left the nettle, he found to his surprise that he was much nearer the top of the mountain than he had expected, and the higher he went the easier the ascent became. He almost wished that the nettle had stung him, so that he might have remembered all the wonderful things in the past that he thought he must have done, if what the nettle spoke was truth, but the thought of the future, that he was sure was yet before him, made him spring forward and upward.

That strange sense of climbing a mountain; the higher you do go, the higher you *can* go, till you feel at last like a feather blowing your own self upwards. And thus Willie felt, and everything opened out before him just like Jack's famous bean-stalk must have opened had you seen it grow bud after bud, flower after flower, leaf after leaf, shooting swiftly up and outwards.

At length the end came in view, the top of the mountain. And it seemed to him to become quite pointed and girt with clouds, like one of those Welsh peaks, right there, alone in the sky, with the valleys lying all about it, north, south, east and west; a sunset and a sunrise view, and mists, floating round, now above, now below.

As he approached the top he saw a figure sitting on a heap of stones that pointed the summit of the mountain, and the figure sat looking to the way of the setting sun.

How strange to meet a man like this on the top of a mountain, and he was all in grey, clothed as the boulders, and the dim red golden light of the setting sun was playing round him, and seemed to claim him as part of the landscape.

" I'll go and ask him the way," said Willie to himself. " He'll know. How solemn he looks, I wonder what he's thinking about, and what he's peering at into the sunset ? "

But surely he knew the figure. Yes! as he come nearer it was unmistakeable, and a few more steps brought him within hearing. It was the old monk. There, all alone on the top of the mountain, he sat dreaming into the sunset, and thinking as he dreamed. A great gladness came over Willie as he drew nearer to him. But the old monk showed no surprise at seeing him.

"So you've got to the top of the mountain, laddie?" he said. "Good luck to you!—have you seen many strange things?"

"Well, yes," said Willie. "Strange people, rather."

"Would you like to see them again?" said the old monk.

"The nice ones," said Willie.

"One can't always choose," was the old man's answer.

"Shall I see them all again? I know I shall see the little lady in grey again, because she promised, and I know she's a sort of person who keeps her promises."

"Yes," said the old monk. "You'll see them all all again—that is, probably, one always does."

This was not quite so nice.

"What! Giant Grumbold, too?"

"Oh yes," said the monk. "He's sure to turn up again—besides, he grows."

"Grows! I should have thought he was big enough by now."

"No doubt," said the old monk. "Other people think so too, especially Mr. Pushington. But he never stops growing—that's his misfortune—and sometimes he outgrows his strength."

"What's does he do then?" asked Willie.

"He waits till he catches himself up again," said the old monk. Willie was a little perplexed.

"Of course his pie grows with him."

It seemed reasonable that a giant should grow, but a pie growing was a new idea. Still, if the pie was part of the giant, and the giant part of the pie, perhaps it wasn't so odd after all.

"Yes," said the old monk, "one always see everything again, and everything always turns up again. It's not always the same as it was before, because, you see, sometimes you meet it when the sun

rises, and sometimes you see it when the sun sets, like now—so it
may be cold, and watery, and blue, or it may be warm, and golden,
and red ; but it always comes again, it always comes again," he
added. dreamily, and then he gazed fixedly at the sunset and began
chanting his old chant to himself, and the words sounded sweet, and
strange, and different : " Good luck have thou with thine honour—
ride on because of the word of truth, of meekness, of righteousness,
and thy right hand shall teach thee terrible things."

The summer sun was sinking through the woods in the valley, the
trees were nodding in response, the plain in its green and golden
colours, had joined in the chant.

Then there was a pause, and everything was silent, simply everything. You might have heard a dandelion seed drop, there as you
sat in the midst of all this vastness. It was as silent as if ten
thousand people were together, and holding their breath to listen
what a great orator was just going to tell them.

The old monk broke the silence. " It's on an evening like this
that they all come back," he said. " Don't you remember the
proverb about casting your bread upon the waters and finding it
after many days ? "

Willie thought he did, though if the ducks eat the bread he didn't
quite see how it could in that case.

" The ducks never eat the bread," said the old monk, interpreting
his thoughts. " They seem to sometimes, but they never really do ! "

Then he began dreaming again, and gazed longingly at the great
sinking sun.

" You don't know how good and kind the sun is, or what it
doesn't all do for us ! Look at it now," he added and he pointed
his withered hand to the West. " See those red streaks of growing
mist—the great arms of the sun as it embraces everything,"

Then he paused, still pointing, and his old hand shook as it traced
for Willie the movements of the clouds as they flowed from the
setting sun, and Willie knelt down beside the old man and watched
with the movement of his hand.

D 2

"The great red sun as it sinks gathers up all the beauty, and the splendour, and the greatness of the world into its bosom, and carries them under, and then what do you think it does with all its treasures?"

"What?" asked Willie in a whisper.

"It changes them into a life of new colour, and new beauty, and new greatness, and brings them up again on the other side on the next day—See!"

And Willie knelt in the evening sun light leaning his head against the old monk's knee. And after they had been there for a while the old monk spoke again.

"Would you like to have a peep into the future?"

"Yes," said Willie.

"Well, then watch with me here for a bit, and as the sun goes down you'll see something."

So Willie watched.

Then the valley below began to catch into light, the trees no longer green began to change into reds and greys, and a strange purple coloured mist rose in the valley, and as it rose two figures seemed to form out of it, both in glittering armour and carrying swords.

Willie was nerved with excitement

"Who are they?" he asked, catching hold of the old monk's sack-cloth.

"Watch!" said the old monk.

"Are they King Arthur and Sir Launcelot? If so I must go to them!"

"No," said the monk. "No! watch!"

The two figures came nearer to each other and little by little Willie could distinguish them in the mist, the one was old and firm, and stately, and wore on his head a great crown imperial set with jewels. The other was young and dazzling and on his head was a red crown.

"It's the two kings come out to fight again." said the old monk.

"What kings?" asked Willie.

"That one," said the old monk, pointing to the stately greybeard "owns the greatest empire that has ever been, the empire on which the sun never sets, and that one," he said pointing to the dazzling youth—"that one rules the empire that is to be."

" What are they fighting for ? " asked Willie.

" The same that all the greatest battles of all time have been fought for."

" What's that ? " said Willie.

" An idea," said the old monk, "and whenever the clash of their swords is heard in the valley and the red banner and the Union Jack come out to war, all the plains and the hills and the woods look on in wonder to see how the conflict will turn and what will come of it all."

" Whose is the best idea ? " asked Willie, "and which do you think should win ? "

" There is no better or best in ideas," said the old monk. " They are all equally good, the misfortune is that to get *one* you sometimes must lose the others, but here the woods and the valleys and the hills live in hope that both may win."

" Which do *you* think will win ? " asked Willie.

" I don't know," said the old monk, " let us wait and see."

And then the clash of swords broke from the valley and the two champions were measured in the fight, and the sheen and glitter of the steel and the gold shot up through the mist and they fought for a long space and neither won, each being equal to the other.

Then suddenly the king of the red crown made a great pass and followed it up and the greybeard was driven back and it seemed he was about to fall and that it would be all over with him, and Willie gave a cry of sorrow for he thought in that moment of all the great deeds of the past, and the great battles and the great men of England and all that he had ever read and dreamed of in his history books, and he thought how this would all vanish with the fall of the king with the golden crown.

" Can nothing help him ? " he said to the old monk.

" Watch ! " was the answer.

And scarcely had the old man said it when the battle turned again; the king of the red crown slipped and the greybeard sprang up and upon him, and none of his youth and splendour seemed to serve him now. It was but a moment and the end would be there, and in that moment the thought came over Willie that all his friendships and all he had been taught and all his dreams for the future and all he had ever loved would be lost to him if the young king fell, and he seized the old monk by the hand and sprang to his feet.

"Let's go and help him!" he cried.

But ere he had said the words a great moaning wind swept across the land, the trees bowed their heads, a grey mist trailed through the valley and both figures were blotted out of sight.

"I must go and see!" cried Willie. "I must go and see!" and forgetful of the coming night or of the unknown mountain ways or of the old monk whom he left up behind him, Willie bounded down the mountain path to seek that strange king in the scarlet crown.

"Remember! remember!" a warning voice called after him. "Remember! remember! you have your own battle to fight. Forget not that you wear the yellow armour, and carry the enchanted sword."

CHAPTER VIII.

TELLS OF WHAT HAPPENS TO EVERYBODY WHO IS ANYBODY IN PARTICULAR.

TO catch a butterfly in a net as you run down hill is one thing. it may be nice for you but it isn't always so nice for the butterfly, because—and Willie had been told this very clearly, —butterflies preferred showing their wings in the open air to showing them in specimen boxes. But it's quite another thing when the butterfly turns round and catches you in the net that you intended for him and sternly bids *you* go into *his* specimen box.

Here was Willie chasing the future down hill as if it were a butterfly and lo! the future turned and closed in upon him.

Faster and faster he ran, and darker and darker it grew in the valley, and denser and denser became the mist, till soon he could see neither the mountain that he had left behind, not the valley that he was seeking before. Still on he ran, scampering over the boulders, jumping from ledge to ledge, following as best as he could the steep winding path that led down the side of the hill. And still the evening grew darker around him—the sun was gone, the mountain was no longer visible, the valley itself though nearer was out of sight. A little space and he was all surrounded in the dark grey mist, and could see no more than the few steps before him as he sprang from ledge to ledge. What if his foot should slip now and he fall down some precipice. Yet the thought of the strong youth with the red crown made him speed on regardless of danger, and forward he sprang swifter and swifter.

He thought the journey was almost endless, he did not know how far he had gone or how long he had been running. At length the ground grew less steep, and he thought he must be getting near the plain, then as ran he felt it becoming sodden, it was marsh land and reeds instead of boulders, and when he was quite on the level he checked himself, stood still and tried to listen and take his bearings.

He could make out nothing through the mist, it was wet, grey night all round him, he listened but could hear nothing. There was no sound of swords or fighting—one sullen silence all about him. Still he felt the impulse to go on, so he went, going in the direction in which he thought the Kings must have been. He went slowly, for it was heavy walking in the marsh, and the mist had so closed in upon him that he could see only a few paces before him. Where was it all going to lead to? Was this the future? How would he ever make his way through?

Suddenly he became aware of a figure standing in the path before him. He looked and it was another knight clothed in armour like his own. Could this be one of the kings at last? Could it be one of his own heros even? Willie's heart beat with joy. But the figure made no way for him. It stood firm. Willie drew himself up.

" Who are you? " he said,

" I am Opposition," answered the figure, " draw and fight me ! "

Willie was prepared—here then was his battle and he had the enchanted sword to fight with. He felt safe and strong. He drew, and stood himself in position. The two swords were ready and the two knights measured in battle against one another.

Willie felt the weight of the strange knight's steel against his, it weighed heavy. The strange knight had an iron arm. They struck and struck again, each watching the other's eye, but the strange knight stood firm as a rock: and all Willie's strokes as he sprang lightly round him did he seem to turn aside as he might turn the twigs in a wind swept forest. There seemed no moving him.

Then as Willie watched his enemy's eye, there came into it a strange glitter. It was an uncertain eye that said " don't trust me " and Willie felt its warning and that he must be on his guard for some sudden attack other than that of the sword.

And so forsooth it was. The enemy was changing; changing form; as his eye so his body, he was growing greater before him; greater than Willie; heads taller than Willie, stronger and more terrible. Willie nerved himself together for a brave assault upon him and after a little skirmishing dealt the strange one a great blow upon the chest. when lo! instead of impenetrable steel with strong flesh and blood behind it there was a sound as of the whole man being hollow from top to toe, a deep empty sound as if something had been smitten that had no substance. Willie struck again and the figure stood erect and motionless for a minute and then all life went out of its eyes, and a voice not of it but from within it cried in a hollow hissing sound—

"Idols—idols—illusion—illusion—idols—ss—sss—ssss!"

"Come out of it!" cried the boy. "Whatever you are!" and he smote again.

Then everything fell to pieces. The great arms fell off with a thud upon the ground, and the head with its helmet breaking as it fell—then the legs toppled over, and the big hollow torso broke open into two.

But a new horror came from within it—coiled in a nest of slime was a big serpent, flat browed, hairy headed, with mottled glittering colours on its skin—and stiff uneven flanges growing from it, horrible to see.

Willie made for it at once as it swiftly shimmered towards him and with his sword struck off its hairy head, instantly two new heads sprang out in its place—he struck again, and two more heads sprang forth, for every head he struck, two new ones, glittering eyed, hairy, and horrible sprang forth. Willie was bewildered. The serpent's heads closed around him—their flanges expanding and contracting, their heads hissing and waving to and fro and coming nearer and nearer on to him till their sickly slime was covering his armour. Then he bethought himself—striking with the sword only brought more—so he would merely stand still and see what they would do if they closed in upon him and he stood quite firm, unmoved. This had its effect. The serpents seemed to grow powerless. They throbbed and hissed against him but they could not strike him, and never a one could stand the look from his face—one by one they shrivelled away and were paralysed—one by one—till at last with throbs and shivering and palpitation the whole was reduced to one black mass and Willie thought the terrible battle was over.

But it was not over. Just as he was preparing to put up his sword and go his ways—the dull black mass sprang into life—darted up into the dark grey air and made for him—it was none other than the demon—the demon now flashing wickedness and fury from his eyes. Willie was no longer attacking, he was being attacked—the demon sprang on him—first here then there—from behind and from in front and Willie struck out lustily with his sword.

When sudden—snap! clash!—glitter of broken fragments and splinters—the enchanted weapon was shattered into a thousand pieces. It was all over with Willie. In an instant the demon was upon him, seizing him by the throat as a dog might, he swung his legs round the boy and sought by swaying himself to and fro to throw him over on the ground and trample on him.

There even in the thick of the closed struggle the thought came to Willie. "That comes of trusting to an enchanted sword—I might have thought those old fashioned things were humbug." And swift as lightning another thought came to him. "Stratford fists will do it though!" and suiting the action to the thought he let fly right and left, bang! bang! bang! on the demon's face, nose, eyes, ears, mouth, as never a school-boy did before. This was the way to beat Proteus. A few minutes and all was over. The demon let go his hold and fell to the ground howling horribly, then he jumped up, turned tail and in terror lest Willie should give chase, scarce daring to look round, and howling with pain he ran helter skelter away into the mist, into the silence, into the night.

CHAPTER IX.

WHEN the demon was gone the mist began to clear. Sky and plain and mountain showed themselves again but dim and hidden for it was night now, and Willie wondered in how small a space the darkness had come over. Surely the battle did not last so long into the night. Yet even so, for there was the queen moon in the sky and the fleecy clouds driving across her as they do when the wind and she are at peace together and he scatters them away to make the night clear for her to shine.

After a while as he went, it seemed to him as if he heard the sound of music in the night far away—that strange plaintive sound of distant singing, like a lingering breath upon the air. He waited to listen whence the sound came, and then made for it. It seemed some distance away in the valley. As he came nearer, it grew plainer. It was the sound of a singing that he knew well, the songs of his mates the other boys. Strange that they should be there! And what could they be doing here in the night. His heart beat for joy at meeting them again where he least expected to meet them, after all his travels and adventures, for what strange things had he not to tell them ; and to be with them—what delight ! For he was weary and worn with the battle and to be with them would be great joy.

Indeed, he looked rather a sorry sight. His hair was dishevelled, his helmet lost and that bright yellow armour all bruised and soiled with dirt, the cloak with the cross upon it creased and torn. He was no more the gay sunbeam of the morning, all dazzling and hopeful, proud of himself and conscious of his brightness.

Suddenly the singing burst upon him quite clear and distinct, so that he could even recognise the voices of some of his playfellows.

Another few steps and he would be with them, when lo! through the trees something glittered in the moonlight before him. Between him and them was a river, strong, deep and silent. How was he to cross this? He stood still at the brink of the river and cast about him as to what he should do.

There was no light but the light of the moon that glimmered through the willows and the tall rushes, but he thought he saw up in a great old willow tree on an eyot in the river some white figures sitting. How strange!—and he seemed to know them—then there was a song again.

> "I care for nobody, no not I,
> And nobody cares for me."

Yes, it was quite certain that was Hubert's voice and there he sat up in the great tree among the leaves, and there were some of the others too. Yes, he could make them out—there was Walter, and there sat Bill, and there Frank, and there Charley, and at the foot of the tree, was a bell tent and a boat moored to the sags. Surely he couldn't be mistaken. He waited to make certain. Then sang the voices in the tree again.

> " And they all flappit their wings and cried
> Caw, caw, caw.
> And they all flappit their wings and cried
> Caw, caw, caw."

Yes, that was Frank's voice without doubt—that little shrill treble one that wanted to be heard loudest at the finish, without doubt it was.

He waited till the end of the song, and then tried a call. His call carried far away among the forest trees, over the face of the river, and up into the sky it seemed, and then he listened—they must have heard it, and sure enough there came an answer back as clear as anything.

" Pirra whirrrrrr ! "

" That wasn't their call," said Willie to himself. " that was a moor-hen among the reeds in the eyot, how odd that they don't hear me."

Then he waited again, and the singing burst on him louder and sweeter than ever—This time all in parts.

> "And the birds of the air fell a sighin' and a sobbin'
> As they heard of the death of poor Cock Robin
> As they heard of the death of poor Cock Robin."

" How jolly it sounds in the night. I'll join in, then they're sure to hear—Why it's only across the stream!" So he waited till the verse came round and then he sang, shrill and clear into the night as loud as he could

> " Who'll dig his grave ? "

and the answer came back clear and shrill across the water and so faded in a chant,

> " I, said the owl,
> With my spade and trowel
> I'll—dig—his graaa—ve "

and then the chorus broke forth from the great willow tree and its branches bent and bowed with the music.

> " All the birds of the air fell a sighin' and a sobbin'
> As they heard of the death of poor Cock Robin,
> As they heard of the de—ath of poor Cock Robin ! "

No, they didn't know he was there that was evident, so he waited for another silence and then tried another call, and clear as ever the cry of the moor-hen among the reeds came back over the night,

> " Pirra whirrrrrr ! "

Willie began to feel lonely and wretched at the thought of being so near to the other boys, and yet quite unable to make them hear him. Then the music beckoned to him again, this time all tripping and dancing to the little Italian tune so well known to him.

> " I knew a comrade true, boys,
> Dauntless to dare and do, boys,
> Loving and gentle too, boys,
> To him a verse is due, boys,
> I sing his praise with you, boys,
> And that for him I'll do, boys,
> What he for me, that I for you, would do, my comrade
>   true ! "

And then again the chorus laughing in the tree.

"Oh, how I wish I could get over to them. It's a cross road I suppose. I wonder if the old monk could help me!" said Willie half out loud.

"The old monk can't help you here," said the kind sad voice.

Willie looked round and saw the bowed figure of the old man standing at his side. His cowl was drawn over his head and he carried his staff in his hand.

"There are some places where no wishing in the world can take you to."

"Can't I swim across the stream?" said Willie, "or couldn't they send the boat over to fetch me—if I could only make them hear?"

"You can't make them hear," said the old monk, "because you see they're in a different world from you—it's they who are in fairy-land now—not you."

"But I'd give it all up to be with them?" cried the boy. "Mayn't I strip my armour off and jump in and be with them?"

"You have donned the yellow suit and you must wear it to the end," said the old monk. "Take my hand and watch and listen."

It was a comfort to have some one for company though he'd have given up the old monk willingly to have been allowed to join in with his mates on the eyot, so he took the old monk's hand and watched and listened.

The night was changing and a cloud had floated across the moon. He could see the figures no longer, only the big swaying mass of tree, but he heard the music and it seemed now as if the tree alone was singing with many voices.

When it was still again, the old monk whispered, "You've read of speaking trees in your fairy tales, haven't you?"

"Yes," said Willie.

"Well this was how they did it. There were the oaks of Dodona —did you ever hear speak of them?—who told men their fates and prophesied the great things of the gods to them—this is how they did it—listen—it's very simple, isn't it?—This is the last time the willow tree will speak to you—listen!"

" Lo, the rolling of the thunder," sang the tree, this time with all its voices fully pitched and the wind of the night making all its leaves rustle and all its boughs rock,

> " Lo, the rolling of the thunder,
> Lo, the sun and lo! thereunder
> Riseth wrath and hope and wonder,
> As the host goes marching on."

Then silence. Willie felt the old monk's palm ticking in his, the pulse of the old man was beating in time with the boy's. They watched together for a while but neither saw nor heard aught, and Willie thought that fairyland had flown again, and that he was merely on the banks of the river in the night.

Then, suddenly the tent shot into light, and he saw the movement of figures passing round within the canvas and the shadows hovering, coming and departing in front of the light and fading on the dim white circle on the tent? Yes it was all there yet, the eyot and the reeds and the willow and the boat moored to the sag, but very dim now, for the only light that showed it was from the tent itself. And then came broken sounds of voices, and laughter, and snatches of song and poetry and jokes—all confused—confused as the shadows.

"Hark! did you hear that?" whispered the old monk.

" No," said Willie under his breath. " What was it?"

" Listen again then."

" Before you came to camp," said a voice in the tent, " came many a welcome gift. Praises and presents came and nourishing food— till at last among the recruits you came, taciturn with nothing to give—we but look on each other—When! more than all gifts of the world you gave me—"

" Hush! don't interrupt! listen again!" said the old monk.

Willie listened but without knowing who's the voice was that was speaking in the tent—and only just able to catch the sound, for it was very still and subdued.

E 2

" Come," said the voice.

> " Come, I will make the Continent indissoluble,
> I will make the most splendid race the sun ever yet
>   shone upon,
> I will make divine magnetic lands,
>> With the love of comrades,
>> With the life-long love of comrades."

Then the voice sank into a murmur and Willie could hear no more, and then the light in the tent was blown out and all was dark as before.

" Good-night," said one voice. " Good-night," echoed another, and the sound sank in a murmur among the reeds.

" Good night ! " " Good night ! " " Good night ! "

CHAPTER X.

IT was like a cold shock to Willie when the light in the tent was blown out. The thought suddenly came to him that he was all and utterly alone in the night, with not a soul to befriend and help him. He felt for the warmth of the old monk's hand, but the pulse seemed to have stopped beating. He held the hand in his still, but there seemed to be no life in it, and instead of being warm it was cold. He pressed it, but it gave no response to his pressure. It was cold, and hard, and friendless. He looked round in the dark, and found, not that he held the old monk's hand in his, but that he was holding the branch of a plane tree that grew at the water's edge, and as he pressed the branch it went lap, lap, lap on to the water.

What was he to do? Where was he to go? The night was cold, and dark, and cheerless, and he had no one to help, or comfort, or guide him. The river he could not cross, the road back would only lead him again over the mountain of facts, and there was no one in the world to help him or tell him what to do. In the darkness there a shiver came over him, and right away down inside him things began to get very creepy and compressed, and like as if his heart was being forced up into his mouth, or wanted to start out of his eyes. To think of this, after all he'd been through; after his great fight with the demon, and his victory! If the demon were to come upon him now, thought Willie, what should he do? And he felt his heart beating, and he had to clench his teeth very tight to prevent the tears from springing.

But somehow the demon did not come, even though Willie thought that this was just the sort of time and place where a fellow like he might take advantage of you.

Willie went along the bank for a bit, down what seemed a rough track by the river, and as he went it was as if everything was jeering at him, and making faces. The trees in gnarled and knotted masks, and the branches grinning and jeering, and the bushes laughing him to scorn, and the wet plants and grasses, as he walked over them, lisping and gibing at him. It was all for this, was it, that he had passed through so much, and seen so many strange things, and as for his friends, it was likely he would find them here, wasn't it?

Forsooth, a pretty knight in his cold and heavy armour, all dented, and with the dew of evening on his face and hair, and the dirt on his hands and limbs! What was the good of it all, *he* wasn't going to find his friends, there were no such things to find, friends didn't exist all. The world was a lonely world, and all that he had done was done for nothing; and then in his wretchedness he threw himself down on a bank of grass, buried his face in his hands, and fairly sobbed aloud.

"I don't think I shall ever find them!" he cried. "I shall give it up! I shall give it up!"

As he said this a voice in the darkness said sweetly and reprovingly to him, "Give it up? Sir Percival never gave it up!"

Willie recognized whose voice it was, and sprang to his feet. In the darkness he peered around to see where the little lady in grey was, and groped about with his hands. Then he felt her little hand stretched to his, and he gave it a great hug, and again he was on his knees before her like a knight of old. It was so good of her to come, and all that way out into the night too.

"Yes," said the little lady, "don't you think ideas can come as well in the night as in the day?"

But Willie could not answer, he was too awed and too excited, all he could do was to hold her tightly by the hand, for fear lest she should leave him again.

And then did she speak words of comfort to him, and told him of great things, and great deeds, and great hopes; told him how every hero had been loyal, and how every hero had kept before him the sunrise aim] that he had first looked to at starting. A hero, she told, was like unto one toiling through a great wood after a golden star that shines to him through the trees, beckoning him onward, who as he goes breaks branch and stem aside that impedes his path and branch and stem behind grow rotten and fall as he has touched them, while branch and stem before grow sparse and thin as he nears them, so that his great golden star shines brighter as he comes towards it till at last he grows bright in the light of his star and loses himself within it.

Willie felt as if he could listen to her for ever, her words were so loving and so gentle. For her sake now all things were worth doing, at her command everything was worth trying. Had she bidden him at that moment toil again and alone over the Mountain of Facts he would have done it. But hers was no stern command now, and all she spake was gentleness.

" What you have loved first that seek to love always," she said, " for where the intention is noble the choice will be noble too. And I," she said, " keep a great book with an index of all names, real names, and name of convenience, and in this book I write down all the loves and the friendships that people have or have had for one another, and when the names and their friendships are once writ in my book no power in Heaven or Earth can blot them out again. And the friends may part, and the lovers cease to love one another, but the record of how they loved first remains, and is a record to their honour for ever."

" But don't mind," she continued, " if when you are down, the trees and the flowers, and even men and beasts gibe at you and make strange faces and look ugly—why faces—there is something in all of them that you don't know—every face has a tale of its own to tell. You do as I say—look at them frontways and look at them sideways, they may be nasty or they may be nice, but there's always something in them that you've never seen before, and that you may always see again."

And thus did she go on speaking and saying strange things to him, many of which he but half understood, though all made him think how loveable she was.

" And now that you've come over the Mountain of Facts," said the little lady, "shall I tell you a secret about something you want ? "

" About my friends ? " asked Willie.

"Aye," said the little lady.

"Oh do, shall I see them soon? Where are they?—show them me please."

"You're quite near to them now."

Willie was delighted. Were they behind the trees there? Was that they in the near distance? Did he see the sheen of their armour in the dim light?—What was it that he saw?—Was his journey through the strange land accomplished?

"Tell me! tell me!" he cried.

"Patience," said the little lady. "Patience. You are on the reverse side of the mountain of facts now, and so the nearer every-thing is to you, the farther it is away.

Willie cried aloud at this, "Oh, I want them! I want them! If they're so near, tell them, do, and let them come to me—they know me—they're fond of me—tell them I've come so far to look for them, and they'll turn and come to me at once."

"Hush!" said the little lady. "Hush! It'll all come right soon. Look!" and she pointed to the sky. "The night is over now, and the dawn is beginning to break. You're tired, you've had no sleep, it'll all be right when the new sun comes out. So rest here a while on this bank of sleeping flowers. I'll watch over you. It'll all be right when the new sun comes out," she added, and taking his two hands in hers, she chafed them, and then folded them across his breast; and then she laid his head gently on her lap, and placed her tender hand first on his forehead, brushing the hair back, and then ever so softly on his eyelids, so that a sweet drowsiness came over him, and he felt he could none other but sleep.

"It'll all come right to-morrow," she whispered, and he heard it half waking, half sleeping, "it'll all come right to-morrow."

CHAPTER XI.

WILLIE did not know if he were awake or asleep. His was
the sort of feeling that you have when you're happy at
waking up and have happy dreams as soon as you fall to
sleep. You like it either way. The little lady seemed to be playing
with him and teasing him.

"Are you asleep?" she said. Yes, he was sure he was. "Well,
then, come with me, and I'll show you everything in dreamland.
But, sure, if you can walk about you must be awake!" and then he
tried to wake himself up in his sleep. "Oh! it's no use trying
that," she said. "That's a very horrid feeling; you'd much better
give it up, because you can't be asleep and awake at the same time,
though you may be a bit of both." So then he thought he was
awake again, and trying ever so hard to get to sleep. "Oh! that's
more horrid still!" she said. "That's what you have in head-aches
and such like things, don't do that. Be either asleep or awake, and
try and remain there."

Thinking he was awake he determined to *remain* so, and fix all his
attention on the little lady, but she laughed at him.

"That, if anything, is the most horrid state of all," she said.
"Now you're like someone who's listening to a very dull sermon,
and feels dreadfully afraid lest the other folk, who are trying to
listen too, shall see him nodding. Go to sleep, boy, go to sleep!
never mind the sermon!"

And when he thought he was fairly off, he heard her say, "Why,
what does it matter, it's all the same whether you're asleep or awake.
Did you ever hear of the musician who composed his great sonata
in his sleep? The story is how the Devil came to him by night, and
taking up the violin that lay by the bedside, played a sonata, the
like of which had never been heard before. When he had finished,

the musician, taking the violin in his turn, played it too, and wrote the music down, and in the morning when he woke, there lay the violin and there the paper with the sonata scored upon it, but he always said that it was not quite the same sonata as he had heard played in the night. Why, people wake up in the morning and think they're awake, they're wrong though ; and then they go to sleep at night and do all their great deeds and think they haven't done them, and they're wrong again. Strange! strange! strange!" Then she waited a bit, and stroked her hand gently over his forehead in time with his heavy breathing, and then, after a long pause, she spoke again, almost in a whisper :

"There was once a wonderful tree on which the five worlds grew, and its roots were in the great river, and at its base sat the three weird sisters of fate, and they tended it at night and bathed it with their tears. And all the day it faded, and all the night it revived again. Aye, it's in the night that things are really awake, and it's in the day that they die and sleep into silence."

Surely the little lady was telling him fairy stories in his sleep.

"Don't you remember the boys singing in the tree?" she said. "There's no mistaking fairyland when you've once had a glimpse of it.

And then her voice grew fainter, and other voices seemed to mingle with hers. "Stuff!" said one, "be practical, what does he want with all these silly fairy tales?"

"Yes," growled another, something like the voice of Giant Grumbold. "Like to know how he's to raise his wages on them."

"That depends what he goes for," said the old monk.

"If he goes for princesses, he'll find princesses, if he goes for wages, he'll get wages, and so if he goes for fairy tales—for wisdom, he'll get wisdom."

"Stuff!" said the other voice. It was the voice of Skugg, the horse-fly, thought Willie. "A tail is a tail, and a fairy—Why, what is a fairy after all? —an improper thing in muslin with sham wings. I hate theatres, they're wrong!"

" Whether by fairy-tales or whether by sarcasm," said the nettle, " You should train his memory more—like the rest of them he's very forgetful."

" Yes," said another voice, this time unmistakeably Mr. Pushington's. " You must train them early, the mind of a boy is like a wax tablet."

" A very wise saying, sir," said the old monk.

" Ahem! yes!" said Mr. Pushington. "I said that in my evidence before the government commission on—on—on—I forget which one —but all the reporters took it down in shorthand and it went right over the United Kingdom in twenty four hours."

Then another voice chimed in also unmistakeable.

" Like wax, like me, like wax, like me," it croaked, " a *black* wax tablet in fact, *black* wax, *black* wax, BLACK wax."

" Sculptor's wax," said the old monk, firmly. "And in the end you see the great bronze statue or the great marble figure of the hero for ever."

" Very true," said the little lady. " There have been heroes all along, and there will be all along to the end; and the best idea I can give you, laddie, is to believe in them straight off, and then be as firm as a rock and as strong as a giant about them."

" Yes," chimed in the nettle, " heroes all along, and I've followed them. I have, from the beginning, and I shall to the end."

" As long as you believe in them," said the little lady again, " you can keep the name of Sir Percival; and remember, remember," she hummed, " it was Sir Percival who saw the Holy Grail, it was he who saw it, it was he who saw it!"

And then a confusion of voices came upon him—and he heard all sorts of things.

" I can bully people in the night just as well as in the day," said the demon. " Black wax, black wax, black wax, ha! ha! ha! tall, *tall*, TALL! and as for you, Skugg, let's be friends again!"

" I will, if you'll spoil it," answered the horse-fly. " Pit it with spots, or scrape it, or blister it, or scratch black pencil marks over its polish, or cut your nasty name on it with a pen-knife, or anything to make it ugly," said Skugg, " I hate vanity!"

"If I can catch him," growled Giant Grumbold, "I won't let him escape again so easily! I'll give it him for getting me into trouble with the boss—insolent young cucumber!"

And then he heard the click of Mr. Pushington's kaleidescope, and all his great machines were booming, and then another click and then Mr. Pushinton spoke, and said, disconsolately, "That's what comes of lingering on the hill! I knew it would be so—now the Union's struck for a rise—on principle—and the Bill's been thrown out—on principle—and the archbishop jumps with the cat—on principle—and the Lord knows what'll happen now—and I did it for the good of the men and the country, and the *Times* called it "enlightened self-interest." Oh dear! oh dear! *all* my screws out again!"

"It's not a bit of use your troubling about me," expostulated the caterpillar, blandly, "you know I shall happen again and again, you should really allow more for the unforeseen—the ever-green unforeseen —really you should, now!"

And then he heard the battling of swords in the valley, and again the two kings had come out to fight, and this time their hosts came with them. Behind the old king with the crown imperial rose all the English heroes: Raleigh, and Nelson, and Henry V., and Edward I., and the Barons of Magna Charta, and Queen Bess, and Sir Thomas More, the great Earl of Chatham, and all who were noblest and bravest in the past, all followed the English flag, and of the other host were men of all nations and types, young men and boys, firm and brisk of step, from distant lands they had come—from the New World and the Colonies, the West and the East, and they sang with a mighty voice the Marseillaise, and pointed to their leader, that strange young king with the scarlet crown.

And then the numbers grew bewildering, and the scarlet crown multiplied itself and began to move hither and thither, swiftly to and fro. And then it changed into a host of red money spiders, who scrambled over Willie.

"A new continent!" they cried. "A new continent! let's exploit it!" and off they rushed out of time, out of space.

" I'm afraid you're having a very troubled night," said the shrew mouse, " if you curled yourself up more in the dead leaves like I do now, you wouldn't be disturbed so much."

" Oh, let him do as he likes," said the elder bush, " can't you leave things alone ?—it's all very beautiful as it is."

And then came a murmur of dissent from the voices beneath ground. " It's all very well for the people that live in the sun," said the beetles, grubs and blind worms. " It's all very well for the people that live in the sun ! it's all very well for the people that live in the sun ! that live in the sun ! that live in the sun ! that live in the sun, in the sun, in the sun, in the *sun ! !* "

And the voices were all drowned in one general murmur, and soon he felt the morning sunlight shining on his face, and the hum of all the insects and the birds, and they sang as they had sung before when the little lady led them, and then one little voice, one little gilded fly among the rest, cried to him, " I'm waiting for you now, stranger. The sun's out, and I've been born—come and see my new wings and share what's beautiful with me ! Come ! come ! come ! "

Then another answered, drowsily, " Oh, let him sleep on a bit yet. . I told him yesterday I had no name. Everything's changed now, and I wouldn't be what I was yesterday—no ! not for all fairy land ! "

And then a stray thing floated by, and he knew it for the dandelion seed, and lo ! the other seed, its fellow, came and kissed it, and then the three—" Three friends united "—they said to one another :

" Stay—we've passed through one æon into another, and now the new world begins again."

And then the little lady in grey whispered to him, " Wake, for your friends are tl ere ! You will find them now ? " and, as she said it, the yellow armour fell off him, first one piece and then another, the casque, and the chain of roses and rings, and the breast plate and the tuilles, till he was standing free and without any let to his limbs, and as the last piece fell off he saw—what ? Aye, what was it he saw? Nothing so very strange after all, nothing that was not quite usual, and as it had always been :—One of the merry boys, his fellows, running by along the road, beckoning to him, and then another boy followed also along the road in the same direction, and that boy beckoned too. And then two others together, with their arms twined round each other, talking to one another as if they had the greatest thing of the whole world to talk about, and as they passed they turned and looked at Willie.

"Come and hear it too," they cried. "Come and hear it too!"

And after them came others, some bigger, some not so big, but he knew them all, all his mates, and he felt he must join them, he wanted to know what it was all about; and there too was Hubert, and there Bill, and there Charley, he must ask them why they had not heard his call to them in the tent, and what they had seen in fairyland on the eyot. And there came another with a big bunch of white pinks in his hands.

"Look!" he cried, "the flowers of June! I've got these on a Mile End stall, have one? Aren't they jolly?" and on he ran.

And then another with his books from school, and then another in his gym-shoes scampering along, flicking his towel and ready for a bathe, and then another playing pitch and toss with an orange as he ran.

"Come along, come along!" cried the last boy of all, "See, there they are, there they are at last! It's a lovely day for a holiday! let's hear all about King Arthur and Sir Launcelot!"

And then a voice of that strange wisdom from the other world seemed to say, "Here shall you see your ideals realized—these be your friends—take the moment as you find it and make it noble, that moment of your life which is brightest and sweetest, that moment which is most real, the moment which in the future you shall look back upon longingly—that is the moment to aim at—you remember how the teacher said ' Whatsoever thy right hand findeth to do, do it with thy might'! Child of the time to be, it is in actual things that your ideals, that the new state of man, the new state of society, will be realized—go and find its fulfilment in heroism."

And away ran Willie with the rest, and as he ran he heard, far away in the distance, the sound of a hymned benediction and the strange voice singing,

" Good luck, good luck, good luck have thou with thine honour, ride on because of the word of truth, of meekness, of righteousness, and thy right hand shall teach thee terrible things."

THE END.

Other Publications by the GUILD & SCHOOL OF HANDICRAFT, or Works issued under its auspices:

THE TRANSACTIONS OF THE GUILD AND
SCHOOL OF HANDICRAFT, Vol. I. Edited by
C. R. Ashbee; Preface by G. F. Watts, R.A.; Lectures,
Addresses, Recipes, by Alma Tadema, R.A., W. Holman
Hunt, Henry Holiday, T. Stirling Lee, E. P. Warren,
Walter Crane, W. B. Richmond, A.R.A., etc.
Large paper copies	10	6
Ordinary copies	5	0
Set of proofs on hand made Japanese vellum, touched by the Artists	10	6

ON SCULPTURE. L. Alma Tadema, R.A.   1   2

AN ADDRESS ON THE OPENING OF THE
WHITECHAPEL PICTURE EXHIBITION.
W. Holman Hunt   1   2

PARLOUR ARCHITECTURE. E. P. Warren. ...   1   2

RECIPES AND NOTES. Walter Crane, &c.   1   2

ON GESSO. W. B. Richmond, A.R.A.   1   2

A SHORT HISTORY OF THE GUILD & SCHOOL
OF HANDICRAFT. C. R. Ashbee.   1   2

DECORATIVE ART FROM A WORKSHOP POINT
OF VIEW. C. R. Ashbee   1   2
Large paper copies   2   6

SOME ILLUSTRATIONS FOR A COURSE OF
LECTURES ON DESIGN IN ITS APPLICA-
TION TO FURNITURE. C. R. Ashbee   1   2

THE MANUAL OF THE GUILD AND SCHOOL
OF HANDICRAFT. Being a Guide to County
Councils and Technical Teachers (*pub. Cassell's*) ...   2   6

A MAP OF ITALY IN THE TIME OF DANTE,
with decorative wood-cuts, hand coloured. Ed. Mary
Hensman. Designed and executed by John Williams,
Guildsman (*pub. Nutt*) ... ...

A TABLE OF THE ARTS AND CRAFTS OF THE
RENAISSANCE   1   2

THE above may be had (post free) of the Secretary of the GUILD & SCHOOL OF HANDICRAFT, Essex House, Mile End Road, London, from whom also information may be obtained as to the productive and educational work of the Guild and School.

www.ingramcontent.com/pod-product-compliance
Lightning Source LLC
Chambersburg PA
CBHW022143090426
42742CB00010B/1366